True Crime

Famous

Murders

&

Missing Persons

Lorrence Williams

Famous Murders

A Stunning Look At The World's Most Famous Murders, Famous Scandals, And Famous Crimes: The Thrilling Stories

Famous Murders

This document is geared towards providing exact and reliable information in regards to the topic and issue covered. The publication is sold with the idea that the publisher is not required to render accounting, officially permitted, or otherwise, qualified services. If advice is necessary, legal or professional, a practiced individual in the profession should be ordered.

- From a Declaration of Principles which was accepted and approved equally by a Committee of the American Bar Association and a Committee of Publishers and Associations.

The information provided herein is stated to be truthful and consistent, in that any liability, in terms of inattention or otherwise, by any usage or abuse of any policies, processes, or directions contained within is the solitary and utter responsibility of the recipient reader. Under no circumstances will any legal responsibility or blame be held against the publisher for any reparation, damages, or monetary loss due to the information herein, either directly or indirectly.

Respective authors own all copyrights not held by the publisher.

The information herein is offered for informational purposes solely, and is universal as so. The presentation of the information is without contract or any type of guarantee assurance.

The trademarks that are used are without any consent, and the publication of the trademark is without permission or backing by the trademark owner. All trademarks and brands within this book are for clarifying purposes only and are the owned by the owners themselves, not affiliated with this document.

Table of Contents

Introduction   vii
Chapter 1: Ordinary People Going On A Rampage To Kill 1
Chapter 2 : Children Who Killed   6
Chapter 3 : Unsolved Murders and Unclosed Cases   10
Chapter 4 : Doctors of Death   14
Chapter 5 : Historical Mass Murders That Shook The
World   19
Chapter 7 : Most Devastating School Shootings   26
Conclusion   30

Lorrence Williams

Want more books?

Would you love books delivered straight to your inbox every week?

Free?

How about non-fiction books on all kinds of subjects?

We send out e-books to our loyal subscribers every week to download and enjoy!

All you have to do is join! It's so easy!

Just visit the link at the end of this book to sign up and then wait for your books to arrive!

Introduction

Life - it is perhaps the most celebrated thing in the world. But what happens if people disregard its importance?

In this book, you will discover some of the world's most famous murders, including who the perpetrators where, why they stole life like it was nothing, and what happened to them afterwards.

You might be surprised at some of the killers because they are quite incapable, until they were... and very much so. The death tolls that are described in this book are boundless, from one victim to a couple of millions.

If you're ready to accept the challenge and you are sure that your heart can take it, turn to the next page.

Chapter 1: Ordinary People Going On A Rampage To Kill

"Who would have thought? These are perhaps the very words that played in the minds of the victims who survived and the witnesses who saw the crimes committed by people who seem to have no guts to perform mass killing.

In this section, you will learn about some of the murders that shook the afflicted community because the perpetrators seemed to have no bad bone to be able to carry out multiple murders.

1. The University of Texas Tower Shooting Disaster

On the afternoon of August 1, 1966, Charles Whitman, an engineering student and a former US Marine, went up the observatory deck of the UT Tower, but his purpose was not to observe, he was there to kill with abandon.

From the 28th floor, Whitman drew out his gun and shot three people inside the observatory. As tragic as it may seem, it wasn't enough for him because from his position, he was able to shoot 15 more students on the ground.

After an hour and a half, Whitman shot himself while

leaving 18 dead bodies and 30 others who were injured.

What's even more terrifying is he killed his wife and his mother in their home before the incident.

2. Eric Borel Family Murders and Killing Spree

At around 6 in the evening, Eric Borel was believed to have a misunderstanding with his stepfather, but no one thought that it would lead to a fatal disaster.

Borel shot his stepfather in the head, and if that was not enough, he got a hammer and repeatedly pounded him on the head as well. Even his 11 year old stepbrother did not escape the tragedy: while innocently watching TV, Borel shot him (again, in the head) and just like what he did to the father, he also hammered him there, this time using a baseball bat.

What's eerie about this event is that Borel seemed calm and collected, going so far as to clean the mess, wipe the blood, and cover the body with sheets. But cleaning it wasn't the end of his insanity.

He patiently waited for his mother to return home, and as soon as she opened the door, he shot her as well, but this time not taking the effort to use a hammer or a baseball bat.

He just packed a bag full of clothes, money, and weapons, together with a .22 hunting riffle, which, he later used to kill 12 more people in the village of Cuers.

Villagers said they never suspected the rifle because it was the peak of the hunting season. And guess what? They mentioned that it was what Borel exactly did: he hunted random people, shot them, and when not properly done, went back to them to shoot again.

In the end, he was able to fire 40 shots leaving 15 people dead.

3. The Xerox Murders

Xerox is a company in Hawaii, United States, and it was usually peaceful until the morning of November 2, 1999.

Bryan Koji Uyasegi, a service technician, went to work as usual, but as soon as he stepped into the building, he pulled out his gun and shot his supervisor. He then shot 6 other people. When the 8th worker tried to escape, Uyasegi fired again, fortunately the said worker was able to get out unscathed.

After the incident, Uyasegi escaped using the company van and was later found sitting there calmly by the Hawaii Nature Center before he got arrested.

Uyasegi's family mentioned that the murderer was having trouble with his co-workers, telling them that they were backstabbing him and harassing him. At one point he was even arrested because he destroyed an elevator out of anger.

The management initiated a psychiatric exam for him and just like a premonition; his interviewer said that he had long since planned the shooting.

Prior to the event, Xerox was phasing out the machine that Uyasegi was accustomed to. He was repeatedly asked to train for the new machines, but he also repeatedly refused. For this, the management said they would have no other option but to fire him.

When asked later why he committed the shooting, Uyasegi just said that; "I am now giving them reason to fire me."

4. The Geneva Country Massacre

It is normal for people to be resentful to others whom they think have wronged them, however, it is not normal to go on a killing spree just for revenge. Such is the case of Michael Kenneth McLendon.

The shooting attack started in the McLendon residence where Michael killed his girlfriend, his own mother and their 4 dogs. After that he even had the tenacity to pack a bag full of weapons.

He drove by his car and went to his grandparent's house where he again killed all the members of the household: his grandparents, aunt and uncle, as well as his cousin.

Still not satisfied, he went to their neighbors and shot the sheriff's wife and their toddler daughter, not to mention a trailer man who was residing in his grandparent's property.

In the end, McLendon did not like the idea of being arrested, so when he was cornered by the police, he shot himself dead.

After further investigation, it was found out that the perpetrator left a list of the people who wronged him. It seemed like he did the shooting for revenge, but the exact reasons remain a mystery, seeing that he killed the people who should have been capable of shedding some light on his behavior.

Chapter 2 : Children Who Killed

Sometimes, the unthinkable happens.

Children are supposed to be the epitome of innocence, incapable of violence and crime. Well, there are instances where kids turn into evil monsters that crave life, and take it by murdering someone.

1. Mary Bell

Who would have thought that a girl short of 1 day into celebrating her 11th birthday was capable of killing another innocent child? Mary Bell strangled a 4 year old boy named Martin Brown on the 25th of May 1968.

Police reported that she had done the killing alone but several days later, she and her friend Norma Bell (they are not related) broke into a nursery school and vandalized a wall, claiming the responsibility of the killing.

However, police took this as a simple childish prank.

That was a very grave mistake.

Why? Because on 31st of July, the same year, Mary and Norma yet again strangled a 3 year old boy, but this time, with much more violence. After strangling him, Mary returned to the body to carve an "M" on his chest using a razor, and then she used scissors to cut his hair and a part of his genitals.

When police officers announced to Mary Bell that they would arrest her for two counts of murder, she responded eerily with "That's fine by me..."

Bell was released in 1980 and was granted anonymity (she was given a new name) so that she would be able to start a new life. The anonymity was supposed to cease when she turned 18, but when reporters plagued her and her daughter's life in 1998, the court granted them (Bell and her daughter) a lifetime of it.

2. Eric Smith

Another murder committed by a child that made national headlines because the perpetrator was merely 13 years old, and the victim was just 4 years of age.

Eric Smith was described by his grandparents as a loner who often wanted attention. On the summer of August 2, 1993, a recreational camp in the local park was held and Eric was encouraged to join it because it would do him good to mingle with others his age.

At the same time, the victim Derrick Robbie, who was only 4 years old then, was also a participant to the recreational event.

According to Derrick's mother, she always accompanied her son when going to the park, but on that unfortunate day, she was indisposed as she needed to take care of Derrick's younger sibling. So when Derrick insisted that the park was really near and he could walk by himself, his mother conceded.

This lead to a very tragic event, for when Eric saw the vulnerable Derrick alone, he lured him into the secluded area, and strangled him to near death. What's even more terrifying is the fact that Eric dropped a huge rock on the 4 year old's head, as if to make sure that he really would not survive the ordeal.

Weirdly, Eric went to the police station not to confess, but to "help" with the investigation. 2 days later though, he also claimed responsibility to the killing. Up to now, Eric is still serving his sentence; his next hearing will be in 2016.

3. Josh Phillips

Another murder that made the headlines was the supposed disappearance of Maddie Clifton on November 3, 1998. The police were so hell bent on finding her, there were flyers given, the FBI became involved, a $100,000 reward was initiated and 400 community people volunteered to help in the search.

Guess what? Josh Phillips, her murderer, was one of the volunteers.

A week after Maddie's disappearance, Josh's mom went in her son's room to clean, only to see that his water bed was leaking. Upon further inspection, she saw Maddie's body. She then called the police and Josh, who was only 14 at that time, was arrested in his very school. His victim, Maddie, was only 8 years old.

During the investigation, Josh said that what happened was only an accident at first. While playing baseball, he accidentally hit Maddie in the eye, making it bleed. When Maddie started screaming, Josh panicked so he dragged her to his room and strangled her with a phone cord, hit her again with his baseball bat, and stabbed her 11 times.

Police, however, did not find him convincing.

Chapter 3 : Unsolved Murders and Unclosed Cases

What can be more frustrating than having someone you love taken away from you instantly, and having no one to blame? In this section we will take a look at some of the world's most famous murders that up to this date remain unsolved.

1. The Zodiac Murders

The Zodiac Killings started with just two victims. 2 unsuspecting lovers peacefully sitting in their car were shot in the Bay Area. After that, things started to go downhill for the police authorities, while the Zodiac seemed to be having a lot of fun.

There were a total of 7 attacks, with 4 confirmed victims and 8 more were suspected. But what exactly made the Zodiac a frustrating case aside from the fact the police were at a loss on the murderer's identity?

It was the taunting letters he kept on sending to the media and to the police. The letters were merely codes, and they were made of symbols that seemed to be undecipherable.

True enough, because out of all the letters that the Zodiac sent, only one was translated into a proper, bothering message. And the beginning translation? None other than "I love killing because it is so much fun…"

At some point the Zodiac even sent bloodied shirts of the victims, just to clear up that he was truly what he announced to be: an unidentified killer.

2. Tylenol Murders

In the year 1982, 7 people in Chicago died after taking Tylenol pills that were traced with cyanide.

It started with just a chest pain, so Adam Janus took a few pills of Extra Strength Tylenol. An hour later, he died. When his brother and sister in law found out about his demise, they were so grief stricken that they also popped a few pills from the same bottle. Not surprisingly, they too died.

From the same neighborhood, a girl was suffering from a cold so she took a few pills of Tylenol, that girl also became a fallen victim.

This brought alertness to the people and so authorities issued warnings so that the public would know of the dilemma.

Upon investigation, the police found out that the bottles were traced with cyanide. What's weird is the fact that those pills taken by the 7 victims came from different factories, but the death toll was only in Chicago.

This led them to believe that one person, or a group of them, took several bottles, traced them with poison, and then returned them to the grocery where they bought them.

From there on, the Anti-Tampering law was initiated: "Do Not Accept If The Seal Is Broken".

3. Ciudad Juarez Women Murders

Perhaps, once of the most tragic mass murders recorded in recent history were the killings in Ciudad Juarez. The killings started in 1993, and up to now, justice is still unserved.

Experts believed there were a lot of contributing factors that lead to the demise of hundreds, and one of them is the cheap labor that often targeted women. During those times, women "migrated" from one place to another to be able to find work, and Ciudad Suarez was a perfect choice because it was near the American borders.

It is believed that hundreds of women were killed; some people even say that there were thousands. The manners of killings are different, and the perpetrators are perhaps, up to this day, still at large.

Chapter 4 : Doctors of Death

While it may sound so mystifying, angels of death are in fact real. And no, they do not involve paranormal activities. The angels of death are real people, disguising themselves as healing angels. They take care of you and help you recover. Well, those were supposed to be the goals of doctors, until they become the angels of death.

In this section you will learn of the three medical professionals that shook the world because of their license to kill.

1. Michael Swango

A smart student and a promising doctor-- that was what people thought of Michael Swango before he turned into an unstoppable killing machine.

It was believed that Swango's only motive in becoming a doctor, was to kill.

While studying to become a doctor, his schoolmates noted how "fatality" excited him abnormally, going so far as becoming happy when approaching the scenes of accidents. However weird that is, no one thought that Swango would chase the thrill of death.

During his internship in Ohio State University Hospital, Swango started to attend to patients individually. One patient was recovering very well from a vehicular accident, but after Swango's swift visit, the female patient was found dead.

He was fired for his doings (there weren't just one), but the hospital, afraid of lawsuits, let him finish the internship without a commotion.

In his job in Illinois, he often gave his co-workers some nice desserts, but after consuming the gifts, they would all fall ill. This time, Swango did not escape the hands of the law.

When he was released after 5 years of his sentence, he did everything in his power (changing locations, and using other names) to have more victims to his name, even poisoning his own girlfriend.

Finally, Swango was cornered in Zimbabwe and was sentenced for a lifetime of imprisonment without bail. It is believed that he is responsible for over 60 deaths.

2. Miyuki Ishikawa

During the 1940s, came a Baby Boom in Japan. That said, there were a lot of babies being born, but their parents were incapable of taking care of them. Due to this, Miyuki Ishikawa suggested to the mothers that they put their newborns under her care, even though her maternity clinic was already overflowing with babies.

Problem is, Inshikawa did not have the proper resources to take care of the innocent newborns. They were taken, placed somewhere within the clinic, but they were not fed.

It was like placing the babies down in the crib and forgetting all about them. Baby after baby, the little dead bodies piled up and the good doctor started disposing of them all around the city.

For years Ishikawa continued the practice, and she even charged parents, telling them that her service was less expensive than having to raise the kids on their own. She and her husband even hired a doctor to falsify the death certificates.

It was when the police accidentally stumbled upon a bag full of 5 dead babies that she was investigated and subsequently, arrested. Ishikawa is believed to be responsible for the death of 160 newborns.

3. Herold Shipman

Herold Shipman was no stranger to diseases-- growing up with a mother that would eventually succumb to cancer. Thus, it comes as no surprise that he would someday become a doctor. And he did.

During his early career he found something fascinating about morphine that he became addicted to it. When he was found out, authorities sent him to rehab but kept his license to practice medicine in tact. Thus, when he was released, he continued to practice medicine, this time as an on-call doctor tending to elderly in the comforts of their own homes.

However, elderly patients in Shipman's care seemed to be always dying. Unknown to the relatives, Shipman was overdosing them with heroin. After the death he would encourage the relatives to cremate the body, ultimately erasing the evidence of his killing.

But because there seemed to be a lot of cremations happening under Shipman's care, the police started investigating. They found out nothing until the case of Shipman's last patient.

The elderly was in very good condition, but she was found dead. Her lawyer son was notified that his mother left a will: over 300, 000 pounds, but not for the family, instead it was left in the name of Herold Shipman. Since the body was not cremated, Shipman was arrested with due evidence.

It is believed that he was responsible for over 300 deaths.

Shipman was imprisoned, but after 4 years, he hanged himself using his own bed sheets.

Chapter 5 : Historical Mass Murders That Shook The World

While it is true that mass killings still happen at present, these cases are not as violent, and as extensive as those that happened in the past. In this chapter you will discover some of the world's most famous mass killings that shook the whole world.

1. The Holocaust

When talk about mass murders ensues, a list would not be complete without the mention of the Holocaust, The German Nazi, and of course, the man in the middle of it all, Adolf Hitler.

Holocaust is a combination of 2 Greek words. One is "Holos", meaning whole, and "Kaustos", meaning to burn. It was originally used to refer to sacrifices to the God. However, World War II prompted the whole world with its new meaning: Mass Murder.

And we're not talking about 10 people, not even a hundred, or a thousand. The holocaust killed roughly 11 million people. The Nazi's openly admitted that the cause of the tragic massacre was none other than Anti-Semitism.

Anti-Semitism is a term used to describe the hostile actions against Jews. According to the Nazis, Jews were lowly individuals; they were aliens that humanity had to get rid of. Clearly enough, they took the honor of doing so.

From 1933 to 1945, The Nazis burnt 11 million Jews, and to make the act more heartless, they started burning those whom they thought were the least useful: the sick, the old, and the too young to work.

2. The Legacy of Mao Zedong

And who can forget Mao Zedong and the legacy he left?

It can be said that Mao Zedong wanted nothing more than a country that could thrive, however, his program, so called The Great Leap Forward left almost 45 million deaths. And although it is quite forgotten by a lot of people, the great famine only happened recently, just in the 1960s.

So what exactly is The Great Leap Forward and why did it result in millions of people who were famished to death.

The goal of the program was to collectivize the agriculture. In simpler terms, private farming was not allowed. The government collected the people's property and tried to use it as land for crops.

While the weather was good, and the harvest was assured, the workers were focused on steel production. Thus, the crops were left to rot, and millions starved to death.

Aside from famine, violence was also rampant during Mao Zedong's era. All who went against the government's will were persecuted.

In the end, Mao Zedong was hailed as one of the most notorious Mass Murderers in history.

3. Joseph Stalin and His Great Purge

Ironically, Stalin was a short man but he stood to be one of the word's most feared murderers. He led the Soviet Union with great paranoia, always thinking that people were out to snatch the powers from his hand. In fact, even his most trusted allies were not safe from his paranoia.

The Great Purge, also termed to as The Great Terror, was centered in "driving away" all the enemies of the people. Apparently, in Stalin's head, more than 20 million were the enemy, because that was the number confirmed by many to have died due to his misplaced proceedings.

Chapter 6 - Famous People Who Were Murdered

Since we are on the topic of famous murders, it is mandatory to mention the people who made news not just because of their success in their fields, but also because of their untimely death. While reading on, you may even remember some of them since they all created turmoil in the world media.

1. Radiation and Litvinenko

While Alexander Litvinenko was no celebrity, he was a highly commended KGB agent. KGB is a military group much like Soviet Army, and though it does not always make news, Litvinenko's death seemed drawn from a spy movie.

On All Saint's Day of 2006, Litvinenko became sick after eating from a sushi restaurant in London. It may have easily been dismissed as simple indigestion, but after three weeks, the KGB agent succumbed to the illness known as radiation syndrome.

It was learned later that while in the restaurant,

Litvinenko was meeting someone for the purpose of receiving evidence for another murder case. Apparently, the tea he was sipping was laced with fatal radioactive substance called polonium 210.

Unfortunately, unlike the movies, no one was convicted of the crime, but many people believed that the Russian Government was involved.

2. John Lennon and His Fan

If you were one of The Beatles' fans, you would surely not forget the death of John Lennon.

Aside from being a success world wide, Lennon was also known by many as someone who loved peace. That was why a lot of people were shocked to know that he was killed, and quite violently at that.

On the evening of December 8, 1980 Lennon and his love interest, Yoko Ono were returning to their hotel in New York when the murderer, David Chapman called Lennon by his name. As the singer turned to the voice, Chapman shot him 4 times.

Amidst the mess, Chapman did not escape. It was reported that he sat by on the street awaiting his arrest. Weirdly, Chapman even had a copy of one Beatles album that Lennon signed on the afternoon of his death.

Lennon was still brought to the hospital but was pronounced Dead on Arrival. Although he was a famous singer, no funeral was held. His body was cremated and the ashes were scattered by Ono in the NY's Central Park.

The reason for the murder is still unknown and Chapman continues to serve his imprisonment.

3. Martin Luther King, Jr.'s Price of Freedom

African American men surely won't forget the prime mover of American Civil Rights Movement. The movement, initiated by King, aimed to get rid of the discrimination against black people.

But, of course not all were happy about the progress.

On the 4th of April 1968 he was dead on the spot. After the event a lot of violent riots took place in more than 60 cities. 5 days later, American President Johnson declared a day of mourning.

And even though it was two months after the killing took place, the authorities were still able to arrest James Earl Ray, a white man who was so opposed to the progress of the Civil Rights that he allegedly killed King himself.

4. Lee Harvey Oswald

You may not know who Oswald was but you surely know the person he killed. That's right, Lee Harvey Oswald was the one who got arrested because he was pointed as the man who killed John F. Kennedy.

Although a lot of people still believe in conspiracy theories, one person took Kennedy's murder quite hard, and he was not happy with the pointed murderer.

So two days after Kennedy's death, and while Oswald was being questioned in Dallas, a club owner by the name of Jack Ruby shot Oswald, instantly killing him.

Chapter 7 : Most Devastating School Shootings

And lastly, we have to discuss the murders that have happened recently: the victims were innocent students and the school staff.

1. The Peshawar School Massacre

One of the most tragic shootings in the history of Pakistan, the Peshawar school massacre led to a lot of casualties, most of them were children.

On December 16, 2014, 7 armed men entered the school and opened fire. A rescue operation quickly followed, killing all the 7 perpetrators and saving 960 people. However for the 145 people who were killed, they came a bit too late.

After a thorough investigation, it was found out that the original target of the attack were the sons of high ranking army officers. Records showed later on, that 50 of the killed students were indeed sons of army officials.

Heroic acts were also recognized after the event,

mentioning that some teachers barricaded themselves in front of their students to protect them.

2. Sandy Hook Elementary School Shooting

And who can forget the shooting that killed 20 innocent children while they were having their lessons?

On December 14, 2012, just 25 minutes after the bell rang; 20 year old Adam Lanza who wore a black mask and a camouflage shirt opened fire. His attack killed 6 school staff and 20 students. After further investigation, it was discovered that before the murder, Lanza killed his own mother at home-- using her own gun. Information revealed that his mother previously taught in the same school.

After the incident, children were asked to close their eyes and hold each other as an adult assisted them out of the doomed building. It was because, by that time, the bodies of the staff and children were still there.

3. Virginia Tech Shooting

One of the deadliest massacres in the world that was committed by just one gunman, the Virginia Tech Shooting will be the last on our list.

To make you realize about how deeply planned this murder was, let us take a look at the timeline and facts.

- On April 16, 2007, at around 7 in the morning 2 police were notified that two victims were killed due to a shooting incident in a coed dormitory within the campus. The gunman, Seung Hiu Cho (who was also a student there, his major was English) was alone. Allegedly, his second victim during this attack was only trying to rescue the first victim.

- After the shooting, Cho was believed to change out of his bloodied clothes. He then went to his computer and deleted emails.

- At around 9 am in the morning Cho went to the post office to send a file that contained photos and videos. The package was addressed to NBC news, however they did not receive it until 2 days later.

- By this time, the school authority had already sent emails to their students that a shooting incident had happened.

- At around 9:45 in the morning, another attack was initiated by the same gunman. It resulted in 32 casualties. A second email was sent by the school to the students, asking them to "stay put" because a gunman was at large within the school.

- In the afternoon, students were already being ushered out and counselling booths were already being set up. The classes were cancelled for the rest of the day as well as the next.

- The gunman shot himself dead.

The package received by the NBC contained photographs of Cho himself carrying guns. It also contained a video that states the shooting could have been prevented. He said (to the Virginia Tech admin) that "You forced me into a corner." He also talked about the wealthy, but nameless people who seem to have everything but were always looking for more.

The victims' survivors received monetary help as well as the injured. Further investigation revealed that 2 years before the incident, Cho was declared to be an "imminent danger".

Conclusion

Once again, congratulations on reading this book.

On a final note, please consider the records here as a collection of the world's most famous killings, but also do not forget that these may be just the tip of the iceberg.

Surely, there are other murders there that will make your skin crawl with fear.

Thank you, and I hope you enjoyed this book!

Missing

Persons

Strange And Bizarre Missing Persons Cases And The True, Mysterious Stories Of Missing People

Table of Contents

Introduction   33
Chapter 1 : Jean Spangler   36
Chapter 2 : Michael Rosenblum   44
Chapter 3 : DB Cooper   53
Chapter 4 : Michael Rockefeller   61
Chapter 5 : Lauria Bible and Ashley Freeman   66
Chapter 6 : Brenda Starr Snouffer   74
Conclusion   78

Introduction

I want to thank you and congratulate you for purchasing the book, *"Missing Persons: Strange And Bizarre Missing Persons Cases And The True, Mysterious Stories Of Missing People"*.

Not all people that have gone missing were famous and powerful-- some of them were ordinary citizens, who lived their lives simply, without complications. So, why would they suddenly disappear? Could it be possible that they were facing battles far more serious than they let on?

Thanks again for purchasing this book, I hope you enjoy it!

and consistent, in that any liability, in terms of inattention or otherwise, by any usage or abuse of any policies, processes, or directions contained within is the solitary and utter responsibility of the recipient reader. Under no circumstances will any legal responsibility or blame be held against the publisher for any reparation, damages, or monetary loss due to the information herein, either directly or indirectly.

Respective authors own all copyrights not held by the publisher.

The information herein is offered for informational purposes solely, and is universal as so. The presentation of the information is without contract or any type of guarantee assurance.

The trademarks that are used are without any consent, and the publication of the trademark is without permission or backing by the trademark owner. All trademarks and brands within this book are for clarifying purposes only and are the owned by the owners themselves, not affiliated with this document.

Chapter 1: Jean Spangler

Hollywood is a dream. An aspiring artist would never pass up on the opportunity to be in a Hollywood movie. The glitz and the glamour are appealing, especially to young women who want their talent and beauty to be noticed. Sadly, not all are given the same wonderful opportunity. In fact, some even disappear while trying to pursue their acting passion, like Jean Elizabeth Spangler.

On September 2, 1923, Jean Elizabeth Spangler was born in Seattle, Washington. Before she disappeared on October 7, 1949, she was a singer, dancer, and a part-time actress in Hollywood films. At the time of her disappearance, she was only 26 years old.

Jean was a divorcee, and she had a young daughter named Christine Louise Benner. Her former husband and Christine's father, Dexter Benner, once had the custody of Christine. Back then , the court sided with him because of Jean's extra-marital affair, and her lifestyle which consisted of partying a lot.

Dexter claimed that Jean's lifestyle would always take precedence before the well-being of their daughter and at one point he even threatened Jean that he could take Christine to a place where she wouldn't be able to see her again. This was the last straw, so Jean took Dexter to court, and finally won over the custody battle in 1948. The court asserted that Jean's wild" life was already behind her and she could now properly take care of her daughter. At the time of Jean's disappearance, Christine was only 5 years old.

Jean and Christine lived in a house in Wilshire District in Los Angeles, with her mother, her brother, and her sister in law, Sophie. On October 7, 1949, at 5 pm, Jean kissed Christine goodbye and told Sophie that she would be meeting Dexter about a late child-support payment (in some reports, it was about increasing the child support). Afterwards, she would be night shooting a few scenes for a new movie. "Wish me luck," she told her sister in law.

When Jean didn't come home the next day, Sophie became distressed. She became so worried that she hurried to the Wilshire Division of LAPD and reported Jean as missing. Although the police collected the details, they were doubtful that Jean was even really missing. For them, she must have just partied hard and stayed out for the night.

They didn't even enter her name in the police teletype for missing people. Nevertheless, they still checked the studios where she worked, but weirdly, each one said that they had no work in progress with her. On top of that, none of the studios had scheduled shooting on the evening of October 7. Still, the police were quite sure that Jean would turn up after a day or two.

Well, they were wrong.

Two days later, there was still no sign of Jean, but her purse was recovered near the Fern Dell entrance to the Griffith Park. When the police took possession of the purse, they noted that the other strap was ripped. This led them to believe that she was mugged, but after Sophie said that Jean virtually had no money when she left, they ruled that suspicion out. Mugging aside, the ripped handle still conveyed violence. More interesting was the note inside the purse. Clearly enough, the note was written by Jean, and it said:

"Kirk-- Can't wait any longer. Going to see Dr. Scott. It will work out best this way while my mother is away,"

The note ended awkwardly and with a comma, so the authorities assumed that she never got to complete the whole message.

Since the discovery of the note, LAPD had assigned 60 people to search Griffith Park, but despite this effort, no other clues came forward except for a sales clerk in a local market near Jean's house who reported that she saw Jean and it was as if she was waiting for someone. LAPD also questioned Dexter Benner, but he denied meeting Jean. In fact, he hadn't seen her since several weeks prior to the case. Lynn, his new wife, backed his story and said that on October 7, Dexter was with her the whole day.

When Jean's mother returned home, she mentioned about a "Kirk" that had been picking up Jean. The person however didn't enter their home even once- he only stayed inside the car as he waited for Jean. The police also searched for the "Dr. Scott", but each one had no records of a patient with a surname "Spangler" or "Benner."

In the heat of the investigation, and probably after the news of a missing starlet spread like wildfire, an actor named "Kirk Douglas" called the police from Palm Springs where he was on vacation. He wanted to clear his name, and did so by explaining that he wasn't the Kirk being talked about in the note. Before the police could even connect the dots, Kirk Douglas offered the information that Jean worked as an extra to a film where he was the main actor.

He also stated that he didn't even know who Jean Spangler was until one acquaintance reminded him of the small role she played in *"Young Man with a Horn"*. He admitted that he conversed with Jean on the day of the shooting, but not before or after that. Despite Kirk Douglas' honesty, many still raised their eyebrows at his "defensiveness".

Could her disappearance be related to her love affair? In *"Pretty Girl"* the last movie that Jean had worked on, she told the star, Robert Cummings about a "new romance". According to Robert, when he heard Jean whistling her way to the dressing room, he greeted her by saying "You sound happy," to which Jean replied that she was because she had a new romance. Robert asked her if it was serious, and Jean said no, but she was having the time of her life.

And then as if there was not enough mystery, one of Jean's girlfriends contacted the police and told them that Jean had confided with her about her 3-month pregnancy and how she planned to abort the baby. This made LAPD connect her urgency to reach "Dr. Scott" and why it was better "this way while her mother was away". At that time, abortion in Los Angeles was illegal.

Again, the authorities did a thorough search for the elusive doctor, but nothing significant turned up. When they started interviewing the night clubs Jean frequented before, they learned of an ex-medical student who was just known as "Doc". Apparently, "Doc" was famous for doing abortion for a fee. Try as they might, this "Doc" was also as elusive.

The only "Scott" the investigators found was the Scotty to which Jean had an affair with while she was still married to Dexter. This Scotty was violent and even threatened to kill her if she left. Scotty, however, made no more contact with Jean since 1945, and he wasn't a doctor but an air corps lieutenant.

The police investigated each place that had even just the slightest connection to the starlet, but came up with nothing. In one interview, one investigator even mentioned that the only thing they found out about Jean was that she "got around a lot". In their quest to find her, they learned that she had been romantically or sexually linked to various men such as an educator, a rich playboy, a nightclub owner, jet-setters, and actors. One prominent personality that became controversial during the case was David "Little Davy" Ogul.

Davy, who was connected to a gangster boss named Mike Cohen, was reported to be missing only two days after Jean vanished. When the records were pulled, the police found that they were indicted for conspiracy. They started assuming that the two simply went away together to avoid prosecution.

This theory was further strengthened by a report from El Paso, Texas, that Davey was seen with a lady who looked like Jean. When the police arrived at the hotel where they were spotted, the staff identified Jean from a photo. However, when they checked the records of the hotel, no room was checked under Jean or Davey. They searched El Paso, too, but no sign of Davey and Jean surfaced.

For years, the police continued their search for Jean, but to no avail. No new clues turned up, although a lot of witnesses said they had seen Jean in various places such as Phoenix, Arizona and Mexico City. Until now, Jean's case is still open and she's still under the missing persons' category.

Due to Jean's disappearance, Dexter was again proclaimed as Christine's custodian. He tried to get Lynn (his new wife) become Christine's legal mother through the process of adoption on the grounds of abandonment, but the jury didn't grant it since there was no proof of Jean's death. Jean's mother was granted with visitation rights, but Dexter often ignored it.

Due to his persistent neglect to follow court order, he served 15 days in jail. In the end, Dexter took Christine and Lynn to a new state and never returned. In 2007, Dexter died at the age of 87. He left Lynn, his wife and three daughters, including Christine who now goes by the surname of Williams.

Many mystery enthusiasts still find things odd in this

case. For example, even though Lynn was able to prove Dexter's alibi on the night of the disappearance, shouldn't there be more witnesses or proof? Maybe Lynn was just covering for her husband... This idea sounded logical when it was later found out that Lyn Benner was formerly Lyn Lasky, ex-wife of Ely Lasky who was close to Mikey Cohen-- the gangster boss.

If you'll remember, Davy Ogul was also connected to Mikey Cohen. The connections were odd. Although it could all be just coincidences, many people believed that the police should have concentrated more on it.

Another thing was Dr. Scott. It was mentioned that LAPD searched for doctors with the surname Scott, but what if Scott was actually the first name?

Other people resorted to formulating their own theories. Perhaps Dexter really had something to do with the crime, and Lynn used her previous gangster connection to cover him up? Or maybe, the man 'Scottie', whom Jean had an affair with, returned and sought revenge? Could it be that Davey was really the new lover, and they planned it all along? The chance of solving this case now is slim, especially since possible witnesses now have fading memories.

Chapter 2 : Michael Rosenblum

Valentine 's Day is supposed to be a joyous celebration for lovers, but in 1980, it was clouded with controversy when a man from Pittsburgh, Pennsylvania disappeared.

Michael Rosenblum was not very typical in the sense of youthful exploration. When he was in high school, he tried and experimented with drugs. While other teenage boys would also develop such curiosity, they would still know when to stop and quit it. Michael didn't. In fact, he became overly attached to illegal drugs. His penchant was taking in heavy pain killers. The addiction was so severe that his parents pushed for him to undergo rehabilitation, which fortunately happened.

Unfortunately, it was unsuccessful.

On the evening of February 13, 1980, Michael's mother, Barbara, noticed that Michael was acting strangely again. When she investigated, she found a bottle of pain killers in his room. Out of frustration and lack of hope, she kicked Michael out of their family home in Baldwin Borough, Pennsylvania. At that time, Michael was with his girlfriend, Lisa, so they left the house together using

Lisa's car.

They partied hard straight after being kicked out, so the next morning, February 14, when Michael woke up to a massive hangover, Lisa encouraged hospitalization. Upon reaching the hospital, Michael declined any form of treatment, so they simply left the hospital and went to the nearest gas station, to refuel. At the gas station, Michael insisted on borrowing Lisa's car and driving it. He left Lisa stranded with only a few parting words-- "Go to my parent's house, I'll see you there in two hours."

Well, those were literally Michael's last words because after leaving Lisa stranded at the gas station, he was never seen again.

The next day, February 15, Barbara and Maurice, Michael's father, filed a missing persons report at Pittsburgh police. During an interview, Barbara even told about her regret in what she told her son. Apparently, when she kicked him out, she told Michael that he shouldn't return until the drugs were completely out of his system and his lifestyle.

In her thoughts, perhaps it would have been different if she simply told him to try again and undergo rehab once more. At that time, she thought that her son would return-- his clothes were still in his closet and his money was still intact in his back account. To Barbara, if ever Michael planned on leaving, he would have told his family because that was the way he was. Same with Maurice: during the time, he believed that Michael would come back. After all, he took Lisa's car and he instructed her to wait at his parent's house.

Investigation immediately started. The Pittsburgh Police Department started looking for Lisa's car, after two weeks of trying and there were still no results, Maurice became desperate. He began his own investigation. He printed out posters, offered reward money, and travelled even as far as California. It wasn't until 3 months later, on May 21, that Baldwin Borough Police Department called Lisa and told her that they found her car in the pound. What was more shocking was the fact that it was there since the day Michael left on February 14.

Maurice was shocked- he couldn't believe that the car they were searching for was so close to them. He also couldn't understand how Baldwin Borough Police Department failed to recognize the car since Pittsburgh police gave a detailed description. The car was sitting in the pound for 91 days.

Reports said that the car was found on River Road just two hours after Michael left Lisa. Two of the tires were flat, the key was nowhere in sight, and the engine wasn't hot. There was no sign of Michael when the police found the car. Pittsburgh Police inquired Baldwin Borough about the delay, and they reported that a day after the car was impounded; they mailed a letter to Lisa to let her know.

Lisa insisted that she never received a letter. To prove their side, Baldwin Borough produced the copy of the letter dated February 15. Still Lisa didn't change her stand: she didn't receive any letter.

According to private investigator Stephen Tercsak who was involved in the case together with Pittsburgh Police, knowing the location of the car right away could have been a game changer. Had they received early info about the car's location, the chances of knowing what exactly happened to Michael could have been higher. For Maurice, it was an obvious cover up for something "more sinister".

His logic was simple-- if they were really serious about letting Lisa know about her car, then they should have tried more ways of contacting her. Being able to send the letter meant they knew of her address, so why didn't they go to her? As for the copy of the dated letter, well, that could be fabricated, right? It was very easy to type a date from the past.

What made Maurice suspect Baldwin Borough more was the two phone calls he received. Both calls were anonymous, but the two callers said the same thing: Michael was arrested by Baldwin Borough Police Department. On the first call, which took place before the discovery of the car, Maurice hung up, thinking that it was just a prank.

But on the second call, which was placed after the car's discovery, Maurice became suspicious. And he became even more suspicious when on July 15, 1980, Baldwin Borough Police Department issued a warrant of arrest for Michael Rosenblum. The warrant was for armed robbery which happened in April, two months after Michael was reported to be missing.

The composite sketch issued by the police resembled Michael in some way, but when investigator Stephen Tercsak made his own interviews with the witnesses, they gave a different description. According to the witnesses, the robber was a "white man", who wore "aviator mirrored sunglasses" which reached the top of the eyebrows and extended down to the bridge of the nose.

With these descriptions, it was apparent that the only visible features of the robber was his forehead and his chin. If that was so, then why did the composite sketch include a man WITHOUT sunglasses, and why did it resemble Michael? For Tercsak, the composite was made from one of the flyers featuring Michael's picture.

And as if caught in the middle of something, Baldwin Borough dismissed the arrest after one week of its issuance. No explanation was given.

This made Maurice seek more help. He wanted to know if Baldwin Police had something to do with Michael's disappearance, so he asked for the help of Attorney General LeRoy Zimmerman. However, Zimmerman only cleared the suspicious police department.

He also said that the notice for Lisa must have been lost in the mail. Their statement said 1) Whatever happened to Rosenblum was still unknown, 2) there was no evidence of foul play, and 3) Baldwin Borough Police did not violate any rule, as well as the Streets Run Auto Boyd which towed and impounded Lisa's car.

But if the following information is considered, Baldwin Police certainly violated some rules: 6 and a half years after Michael disappeared, Maurice received an anonymous letter that encouraged him to talk to Margaret Haslett because she knew something about the incident with Lisa's car. Maurice did just that: he contacted Margaret and she did have a disturbing revelation.

According to Margaret, two or three months after the

vehicle was towed and impounded, the chief of police, Aldo Gaburri asked his clerk, Fred Cappelli to write a notice addressed to Lisa about her car. He also asked Fred to backdate the letter to February 15. When Maurice asked Fred Cappelli, he corroborated Margaret's story. He said that at that time, he thought nothing of it.

The chief was his boss, after all. He also added that Aldo Gaburri asked him to deliver the letter to Chester Lombardi (the Senior Officer at the River Road during the scene-- he was the one who found Lisa's car) and have him sign it. Chester didn't agree to sign the letter because it was backdated. When Fred told the chief about it, he just asked him to sign the name of Chester, and not send it. Just keep the letter there.

Angered by this information, Maurice demanded an investigation. When the hearing was over, Gaburri was dismissed from his position, but he contested it. Frustratingly so, he was reinstated and was supported by the Civil Service Commission. For them, there was no "misconduct". The transcript of the hearing was never released, but it was very clear that they chose not to believe Fred Cappelli.

According to Fred, it could be because Gaburri had friends in the council. Civil Service admitted that there were "innuendos" on how the case was handled, but the decision was based from what was presented during the hearing. Later on it was revealed that the one who sent the anonymous letter to Maurice was George Galovich, who was a police officer in Baldwin. He was fired due to "lying under oath" during the case, but later on, he was also reinstated.

A bone fragment and clothes were found on River Road on April 1988. Although the bones couldn't be identified, the clothes eerily resembled what Michael wore when he disappeared.

Could there really have been a cover up? For Maurice, there was. In fact, in 1989, he received a phone call from a person who claimed to have seen Michael in jail at the time of his disappearance. He said that he was Michael's jail mate and he saw that Michael was beaten, probably even shot. He was arrested due to driving under the influence (of drugs or of alcohol, it wasn't mentioned). After some time, the police took Michael away. Back then, he thought they were going to bring him to the hospital but Baldwin Police denied any arrest made for Michael.

In 1992, the proof of Michael's death emerged. A hiker found a human skull near River Road. When the authorities checked, it was positive- the skull belonged to Michael. 12 years of searching was finally over, but the case is still unresolved. Michael's family still ponder on

Lorrence Williams

how Michael died and if he was murdered.

Chapter 3 : DB Cooper

DB Cooper was not a good guy. He was a man not only known because of his mysterious disappearance, but also because he hijacked a plane and demanded $200,000, in exchange for the passengers' safety.

On November 24, just one day before the Thanksgiving of 1971, people rushed to Northwest Orient Airlines, trying to buy tickets for Flight 305. The flight was supposed to be ordinary, as with any other flights. From Washington, the plane would have stops in Minnesota and Montana; finally, it would land on Portland, Oregon for its last flight before hopping to Seattle, Washington. What was so special about Flight 305 was Dan Cooper- the hijacker.

Like other passengers, Dan also lined up for his $20 ticket. At a glance, there was nothing wrong with him, nothing suspicious. He wore a black suit over a white shirt, and his tie was bound by a mother-of-pearl clip. From the two flight attendants who spent most time with him, the FBI found out that he was in his 40's, approximately 77-82 kilograms in weight, and 1.78 to 1.8 meters in height. Others who saw him also gave the same description.

Additionally, he was wearing a raincoat, a pair of sunglasses, and loafers. From these, the FBI had deduced that he looked like a typical businessman, so people didn't think twice about his motives. His ticket was paid in cash and he was not required to submit a photo ID. When he boarded the plane, he was seated on Row 18-- the last row in Flight 305 which was a Boeing 727 aircraft. Even though tomorrow would be Thanksgiving, the plane wasn't full. In fact, there were only 37 passengers. Everyone expected the flight to be uneventful, except of course, Dan Cooper.

Once Dan was seated, he ordered drinks, particularly whisky and 7-Up. He then smoked one of his Raleigh cigars. His order was handed out to him by a flight attendant named Florence Schaffner. Florence also sat down beside Dan as the plane took off. When Dan paid for his order, he handed a note to Florence. Assuming that the note was another flirtatious letter (as Florence was accustomed to), she placed the note in her purse. Dan caught her attention by whispering: "Miss, you might want to read that note. I have a bomb."

Shocked and confused, Florence read the note. The message was written using a felt pen and it said: I HAVE A BOMB IN MY BRIEFCASE. I WILL USE IT IF

NECESSARY. I WANT YOU TO SIT BESIDE ME. YOU ARE BEING HIJACKED. According to Florence, Dan opened his briefcase to show her he was not lying.

What she saw were cylindrical tubes: four were lying on top of another 4. The tubes had insulated wires in the color red and were connected to a cylindrical battery. When Dan was satisfied that Florence knew he was not kidding, he closed the case and dictated his demands for the safety of the plane and the passengers. The demands were: $200,000 "in negotiable American currency", 4 parachutes: 2 were primary and the other 2 for reserve, and a fuel truck in Seattle to refuel the plane once it arrived there.

Florence, went to the cockpit and told the pilot about Dan's demands. The pilot asked another flight attendant, Tina Mucklow to sit beside Dan to keep an eye on him and not let him do anything that would harm the passengers. When Florence and Tina returned, Dan Cooper was already wearing his shades. Florence alerted the pilot of this, and also warned the other flight attendants.

When the captain of the plane, William Scott, received the note from Florence, he alerted the Northwest Orient of their situation. He initially put the plane on hold, by flying around Seattle for over an hour. While William navigated the plane, the officials in the Northwest Orient contacted the authorities to raise the money.

They were able to accumulate $200, 000 in the form of 10,000 $20 bills. Most of the money came from the Federal Reserve Bank of San Francisco, that was why most of the bills had serial numbers beginning in letter L. Most of the bills also had a designation of "Series 1969-C". The authorities hoped that since there were a lot of dollar bills, Dan would have a hard time to escape. Lastly, as an attempt to track down Cooper after the ordeal, they photographed the money.

Due to the holding patterns that William did, the passengers became confused. So as not to worry them, he said that the runway just needed clearing but all else was under control. Finally at 5:24 pm, the authorities signaled William that it was okay to land. The runway had a lot of floodlights that Dan Cooper demanded the cabin lights to be turned off.

He asked this because he was scared that there were snipers waiting to be aimed at him. When the planed landed, the rolling staircase was put down and it was Tina (the second flight attendant) who made the trips up and down to collect the money and the parachutes.

When Dan was satisfied with the money and the parachute, he asked all the passengers to leave, as well as

Florence and another flight attendant. The only ones left on the plane were William, Tina, the co-pilot Rataczak, flight engineer Anderson, and of course, Dan. As they refueled, Dan asked William to direct the plane to Mexico, to which William said that they would need to refuel again in Reno, Nevada.

Dan didn't comment on that. He didn't even ask about flight route. During an interview after the ordeal, William said that everything went smoothly. It was as if Dan was calm, and he didn't want to hurt anyone. As long as his demands were given, then nothing would go wrong.

At 7:40, the Boeing 727 took off again, but this time, there were two fighter jets that tailed them from behind. One was above and one was below-- Dan had no idea about this because he couldn't see the jets. After the take-off, Tina was instructed by William to stay with them in the cockpit. Dan didn't refuse, but Tina noticed that he was tying something on his waist.

At 8:00 pm, the crew noticed that the aft door was open. It was already 10:15 when the Boeing 727 landed in Reno Nevada, but Dan Cooper was nowhere in sight. When the plane landed, police spread out outside the plane, because they still weren't sure if Dan had left or not. After they searched, it was confirmed that Dan Cooper was no longer on board. Apparently, Dan stepped out of the plane with his parachutes and since then, he was never seen again.

After the hijacking, almost a thousand men became suspects. Some of them even claimed to be Dan Cooper, but later on, they were proven wrong. One of the most prominent suspects was Richard McCoy- a Vietnam War Veteran with great parachuting experience.

The FBI reiterated that Richard was not Dan Cooper simply because the descriptions of Florence and Tina didn't fit his physique. Richard was also a political science student, and a few months after Dan organized the hijacking, he also did something similar. The difference was, he was caught and sent to prison. In the year 1974, he died after a shoot-out in a prison break.

In an interesting twist of events, 9 years after the hijacking, one boy who was innocently walking down the Columbia River saw $5,800 dollars in $20 bills. It was confirmed that those bills were part of the ransom provided to Dan to release the hostages. But nothing more came forward after that.

In 2001, the clip on tie Dan was wearing was recovered and from there, the police were able to take a DNA sample. The problem was, there were two small DNA samples and a large one-- it was hard to confirm which one was Dan's or if Dan's DNA was even on the tie.

Perhaps, Dan intentionally placed other DNA there. The case was reopened in 2008 and in 2011, when a woman named Marla Cooper reported that it was her uncle who did the crime.

According to Marla, for 40 years, their entire family swore to protect Dan Cooper, who really was Lynne Doyle Cooper in real life. But her guilt made her come forward. She provided the police with photographs of Lynne Doyle as well as a guitar strap for fingerprints. According to her, the reason why Lynne Doyle used "Dan Cooper" was because it was his favorite comic character.

When the test results came in, it was found that there were no fingerprints on the guitar straps. When Lynne Doyle's DNA was examined, they couldn't find it to match the ones on the clip on tie. The police, however, said that they found nothing inconsistent with Marla's stories, so the possibility of LD being Dan Cooper was still being looked into.

Aside from being missing, D.B. Cooper also raised a lot of questions: the first being his experience in skydiving. Many expert parachutists said that jumping from the plane at the height of 10,000 feet was dangerous for a first-timer. They insisted that if it was his first attempt, then he would have died.

However, if he had prior experience (6 or 7 times), then there would have been no problem. The only factor to consider was if he would have survived the cold after landing. Since there was no body and parachute found, people assumed that he lived. The reason why it became a major issue was because of his actions in the plane.

For the experts, asking for a primary and reserve parachutes was a novice thing to do, but then again, he turned down the offer of an instruction manual. The way he fastened the chutes as what was observed by Tina was an expert behavior, but actually choosing the reserve chute (which was sewn closed and non-functional) was a thing only a novice would do. So, was Dan an expert skydiver, or not? If not, then where was the chute and the body?

Chapter 4 : Michael Rockefeller

The disappearance that rocked the year 1961: the case of Michael Rockefeller. Back then, the 23-year old Harvard graduate had a lot of good things ahead of him. He was an upcoming photographer and an art collector. On top of that, he was one of the heirs of the Rockefeller fortune who was a prominent family back then. His father was also the New York governor at that time, and later on, became the vice president Nelson Rockefeller.

Michael was the fifth and last child of May Todhunter and Nelson Rockefeller. Considering his academic standing in Buckley school in New York and in Phillips Exeter Academy in New Hampshire where he was a student senator, his parents knew that he would go far.

And this expectation was sealed when Michael graduated cum laude in Harvard University. His degree was Bachelor of Arts in History and Economics. After his graduation, he spent 6 months in the US army before setting out for the adventure of a lifetime-- which was also his penultimate voyage.

The trip was supposed to explore the Dani tribe which

was located in western Netherlands in New Guinea, but in the middle of the trip, Michael, along with a friend, temporarily left to explore the Asmat tribe, who were native in the Southern Netherlands. The Asmats were primitive people who lived their lives now the same way they lived it 10,000 years ago.

After having a taste of the Asmat culture, Michael returned to their original trip and went home. The richness in their culture and ethnicity drew Michael in, so much that he returned in the Southern Netherlands to know more about the Asmat and to collect Asmat arts. In his letters while in the expedition, he said that that he was having an exhausting and yet very exciting adventure.

On November 17, 1961, however, the explorations came to an abrupt end when Michael suddenly disappeared.

On that day, Michael and a Dutch Anthropologist named Rene Wassing rode in a 40-foot canoe. They were approximately 5 kilometers away from the shore when the canoe was swamped and was overturned. Two of their guides tried to help, but the help came slow.

Michael and Rene clung to the overturned canoe for some time (about two days) before Michael decided that "he could make it", which meant that he planned on swimming back to the shore. The authorities didn't know if Michael realized how far they were from the shore back then, but from their investigation, it seemed like they were 12 kilometers away when he attempted to swim. The next day, Rene was rescued. Michael, on the other hand, was never seen again.

The search lasted for two weeks. It included planes, boats, and on-foot searchers, but Michael's body was never recovered. There wasn't even a trace of him. Many people believed that he drowned or was eaten by sharks. Although this theory was very logical, how come not one trace was found?

Back then, the news was a headline, what with Michael's parentage, but even this fame didn't help his case. Three years after he disappeared, Michael was declared legally dead, but that didn't mean that his case stopped baffling people.

It remains to be one of the most unresolved mysteries. It's very intriguing that a journalist named Mitch Machlin started to do his own investigating. In 1969, 8 years after the fact, he went to the Southern Netherlands in New Guinea to follow the steps that Michael took. For him, the possibility of Michael being murdered was high.

According to Mitch, if Michael was able to swim successfully to the shore (which was possible because he was a good swimmer and was in good physical condition), he would have landed in Otsjanep village. The history entails that several leaders of this village were killed by the Dutch patrol back in 1958.

It was possible that when Michael arrived there, they saw him as an avenue for revenge because he was a "white man", similar to the Dutch people. It was true that head-hunting and cannibalism were still in practice in the year he disappeared, but for the Asmat people, it wasn't an indiscriminate action. They wouldn't do it unless for revenge.

According to Mitch, in his journey, a Dutch priest named Cornelius van Kensel, said that he heard of the same rumors coming from the tribesmen themselves. Mitch's theory was further sealed by the book published in 2014 by Carl Hoffman entitled *Savage Harvest: A Tale of Cannibals, Colonialism, and Michael Rockefeller's Tragic Quest for Primitive Art*. According to the book, the killing took place and all men in the tribe participated in the murder so as to avenge the death of their tribe leaders.

However, in 1969, another twist happened. A photograph showing a white man amidst a black tribe people, circulated. Sceptics of the "murder for revenge theory" sided with this one-- perhaps Michael became one of the tribes he grew to love. After all, why would the Asmat kill a person who had been doing his research and art-collecting with them?

Perhaps the tribe took Michael and made him a "white idol". Even Mitch, who was a firm believer that Michael got killed, said that he could have survived, and instead of being eaten or murdered, he was turned into a deity. According to him, Asmats, as well as other primitive tribes, considered white people as "wielders of powerful magic".

They worshipped Western goods, like canned and processed food, medicine, weapons and clothing. If Michael landed on the Asmet region, and told the tribe about who he was, they could have considered him as "Godly". Who knows?

Chapter 5: Lauria Bible and Ashley Freeman

Lauria and Ashley were friends since they were in kindergarten, so it wasn't surprising that they wanted to celebrate their birthdays together. On December 30, 1999, it was Ashley's 16th birthday so Lauria decided to spend the day with her and her family which included Ashley's father, Danny, her mother, Kathy, and her boyfriend, Jeremy.

The celebration took place in the Freeman trailer home. The home had no running water, and it was only heated by a wood-burning stove. Apparently, the Freeman family was of the outdoor-types: they enjoyed hunting and preferred to live in an area away from populated communities.

Although the trailer sounded simple, it was still well-equipped with electricity and phone service. Inside the trailer were firearms used by the family because they often went hunting for their food.

According to one of his interviews, Jeremy said that he met with the girls in Wal-Mart. In there, he gave his gift to

Ashley: it was a silver chain, with a heart-shaped pendant. The pendant had Ashley's birthstone embedded on it. After meeting in Wal-Mart, they went to the Freeman's trailer home and spent sometime with the Freeman family and relatives.

Jeremy said that he left at about 9:30, but other relatives said that it was already 10:30 when he departed. Despite this time confusion, Jeremy insisted that nothing was wrong during the party. All of them expected things to be over without any "crime" or "mishap".

In fact, Kathy planned on taking Ashley to her driver's test the next morning, and Lauria, although she planned on staying the night with the Freeman's, had a dental appointment the next day so she promised her dad that she would return before noon.

She never did.

Sometime, during the night, the trailer became an inferno. By 6:00 am, a motorist saw the fire in the trailer and reported it. When the authorities came, the home was already burned to ashes. Inside, a body was recovered and they confirmed that it belonged to Kathy Freeman.

Oddly though, she died before the fire because a gunshot wound was found in her head. Other than her remains, the police didn't find anything else. They assumed that

Danny killed his wife and took the girls with him.

But upon closer investigation, they found out that all of the family vehicles were nearby, even Lauria's car was there with the key in the ignition. The police also ruled out robbery because Lauria's case was found inside the trailer and it still contained the $200 she had.

The next day after the fire, while hoping that they would find more evidence, Lauria's parents, Laurene and Jay Bible visited the scene. Within just five minutes of walking around inside the trailer, they found another body. When the authorities examined it, they found out that it was Danny's body. And creepily, he was also shot in the head. According to Jay the remains were covered with debris, so it was overlooked by the police. When further tests were made, they found out the Kathy died at about 5:00 am. Perhaps whoever the perpetrator was, he or she intentionally burnt the trailer to get rid of any evidence.

Despite Danny's death, he was still investigated. According to Laurene, Danny had a bad temper and short patience. In fact, her daughter, Ashley, was trying to save for a car, but because she wanted to purchase a different car from what Danny wanted, they had a row.

Danny was also accused of abusing his own son, Shane in 1998, but he was acquitted in 1999. Throughout the allegations, Danny was firm that he didn't abuse any of his children. As for the money that Ashley was saving, Laurene said that she finally saved a total of $1200 in the bank, but according to Jeremy, she already had $3000 to $4000.

He also reported that Ashley had no bank account so she kept her money in a plastic container inside the fridge. Upon inspection of the burnt trailer, they found no trace of the money.

Another angle the police looked into was Shane's case. In 1998, Shane was caught driving a vehicle that he stole. When the deputy in charge, David Hayes, asked him to stop, Shane "reached behind him" as if pulling out a gun. Due to this David fired at him and he was killed.

Danny tried to appeal to the court that his son was wrongfully killed, but upon investigation, David's actions were found to be justified. Danny still persisted that Shane was fired at indiscriminately, so he planned on filing a wrongful death lawsuit. Back then, David's brother was also in law enforcement so the two of them took the polygraph test, which they passed. They also withdrew from the investigation, so the Oklahoma State Bureau Investigation took charge.

Some people suspected that it was Ashley who killed her

parents. According to theories, perhaps Danny had been sexually abusing his daughter so she retaliated, or Ashley finally got fed up with her father's bad temperament. Maybe, Ashley asked Lauria for help. However, according to the police, none of the girls' records showed that they were capable of such a violent crime.

Ashley, for one, was even a member of the National Honor Society while Lauria was an excellent student. Ashley almost always partook in sports, particularly in basketball. Lauria was planning on becoming a cosmetologist after graduation. All in all, both the girls had clear backgrounds.

Could it be drugs? According to some unaccounted reports, Danny was involved in small time drug dealing, particularly marijuana. Perhaps, he angered the wrong person which resulted in his and his wife's deaths, as well as the disappearance of the girls. In fact, there were reports about Danny's meeting with two unidentified men 2 weeks before the fire.

The rest of the Freeman relatives still believed that it had something to do with the feud over Shane's death. In fact, Dwayne, Danny's brother revealed that Danny had a premonition of what was to happen. According to Dwayne, before the incident, Danny talked to him seriously and said that "If anything happened to me, look at the Sherriff's Department".

Dwayne confided that the deputies were trying to intimidate the family-- Danny once said that the deputies (David Hayes and his brother), told him that they could do anything to him and his family and Danny couldn't do a thing about it.

Lauria and Ashley's case was even featured in "What Really Happened" back in October of 2001. The relatives of the family participated in the un-purchased and un-aired show. Aside from them, DeAnna Dorsey also contributed. DeAnna was the nurse in the hospital who helped revive Shane when he was shot. Her daughter was also a friend of Ashley's.

Shortly after returning from the taping, DeAnna was shot and killed in the hospital where she worked. According to police reports, the murderer was the paranoid-schizophrenic Ricky Martin who was angry because of the hospital's decision to downsize. People found it odd that shortly after DeAnna's murder, Ricky was also killed by the police.

And what more, friends and relatives said that Ricky and DeAnna didn't know each other. They hadn't even met once in their lives. Could DeAnna's murder really have something to do with her participation in the "What

Really Happened" show?

During the investigation, two people surfaced and claimed that they were involved in the murder and in the girls' disappearance. One was Tommy Lynn Sells, who, in 2002 sent a message to *The Joplin Globe* and said that he had a vague recollection about a fire and a burial of two girls.

According to him, on the evening of December 30, 1999, he planned on returning from St. Louis, Missouri, but he had to first pass through Welch, Oklahoma (where the Freemans were located). He recounted that at that time, his mind was clouded because of drugs, but he "wanted" to recall a memory about a fire and burials for two girls.

Looking into his records, police found out that Tommy had been linked to 16 homicides and most of his victims were very young girls. However, no sufficient evidence could link him to Lauria and Ashley's case.

Another suspect was Jeremy Jones. He was in jail due to his prior murders, but was released at 10:30 on the evening of December 30-- the date of the disappearance. According to authorities, Jeremy Jones used the same M.O. in his previous murders: he shot the victims in the head and then set the place on fire.

He wasn't charged with anything involving the Bible-Freeman case, but he soon returned to prison. In there, he confessed to the killing of the Freeman couple, and then he said that he took the girls to Kansas, shot them, and buried the bodies in a mine shaft near Galena. He said that he did it as a favor to a friend involved in drugs.

Police searched the mine but nothing came of it. In the end, Jeremy Jones denied killing the girls. He admitted that he just confessed so that he could have more "privileges" in jail.

Ashley and Lauria's case, up to now, is still unsolved.

Chapter 6: Brenda Starr Snouffer

On April 21, 1995, a 32-year old woman from Palm Harbor, Florida went missing. Case files described her as Caucasian with blonde hair, blue eyes, and ears that were both pierced. Her whole name was Brenda Snouffer, but the police chose to include her maiden name as she might use it to identify herself especially since she was in the process of a bitter divorce at the time she disappeared.

Brenda Starr Snouffer didn't get along well with her then husband, Scott Irvine Snouffer. According to records, Brenda was supposed to testify against Scott and his brother, Stuart about their "chop shops".

In her statements, Brenda reported that Scott and Stuart dissembled cars that were stolen, so that they could take the parts and sell them. The hearing should have taken place later the same year, if only Brenda didn't disappear. On top of the chop-shop accusation, Brenda and Scott were also having custody battles for their 6 year-old daughter named Mariel.

On April 21, 1995, Brenda's day began as usual. She took Mariel to her school at Highland Lakes Elementary at around 9:15 am. She used her car- a 1993 *Mazda Protege*, which was turquoise blue in color and bore the license plate number LEA14U. After dropping her daughter off, Brenda never returned to pick her up. According to Mariel's teachers, they waited three hours for the absent mother before making a report to the authorities.

The police, of course, immediately suspected Scott, after all, the couple was estranged. However, aside from telling the police that he was innocent, Scott did nothing else to help search for the mother of his child. He just hired an attorney and that was it. In turn, the police never removed him from their list of suspected people.

Apparently, before the disappearance, Brenda confided to her family and friends (as well as to the diary she had written a day before she disappeared) that she was afraid of Scott because he was "threatening" to kill her. To make matters worse, on the day she disappeared, threatening letters were sent to her home, and to the home of one of her friends (Sonny Randall) in Ohio. The letters said: "You have taken everything from me. What goes around, comes around." The sender of the letters, however, was not identified.

When the letters were inspected, the authorities looked into "intentional" disappearance. Perhaps Brenda got fed up with all the stress and pressure of testifying and custody battle, that she fled. For some of the investigators, the letters were so perfectly aimed at Scott, as if someone was deliberately framing him. They also said that they found stationary materials in Brenda's room which was purchased on April 20.

Mariel, remembered shopping for those materials with her mother, and she also added that Brenda withdrew $4,000 the same day. For Brenda's relatives, she wouldn't just disappear without notification-- it simply wasn't her. Besides that, she had a good job as a Registered Nurse in Palm Harbor. She also made plans for the next day which was to take Mariel to Orlando, Florida. Brenda was even planning on visiting Disney World and Sea World.

And the most important of all, she would never leave her daughter behind. Police authorities believed that there was foul play in this case-- but they seriously lacked leads. They even used a helicopter equipped with heat-sensors to see if Scott was hiding her in his 700-acre home, but it turned out negative.

Due to Brenda's absence, Scott's hearing was delayed, but in the end, he was charged with the crimes of automobile theft and possession of an illegal driving license. The jury convicted him to serve only 45 % of the supposed 9 years in prison, and after his release, he would have to be in probation for 7 more years. Stuart, his brother, wasn't charged with anything. The police couldn't collect enough evidence to link him with his brother's crimes and without Brenda's statements, it was impossible to pin him down.

On May 1995, Brenda's marriage to Scott was finally nulled as the divorce was finalized. Even through her absence, she was still awarded with sole custody of Mariel. The jury named her mother as the guardian. However, later, Scott was also able to obtain Mariel's full custody, so his parents took charge in Mariel's case.

Conclusion

Thank you again for reading this book!

An aspiring starlet, a drug addict, a skyjacker, a primitive art collector, two childhood friends, and a simple mother- - the cases we have discussed are still unsolved up to now. No one can say for sure if they will ever be settled. Some could involve foul play, while others could be intentional. In the end, all we have are baffling clues.

I hope you enjoyed this book, thank you and good luck!

Want more books?

Would you love books delivered straight to your inbox every week?

Free?

How about non-fiction books on all kinds of subjects?

We send out e-books to our loyal subscribers every week to download and enjoy!

All you have to do is join! It's so easy!

Just visit the link below to sign up and then wait for your books to arrive!

www.LibraryBugs.com

Enjoy :)

www.ingramcontent.com/pod-product-compliance
Lightning Source LLC
Chambersburg PA
CBHW050425290526
45786CB00003B/1404